LIVES AND TIMES

Dr. Seuss

Wendy Lynch

First published in Great Britain by Heinemann Library,
Halley Court, Jordan Hill, Oxford OX2 8EJ,
a division of Reed Educational and Professional Publishing Ltd.
Heinemann is a registered trademark of Reed Educational & Professional Publishing Limited.

OXFORD MELBOURNE AUCKLAND
JOHANNESBURG BLANTYRE GABORONE
IBADAN PORTSMOUTH NH (USA) CHICAGO

Designed by Visual Image
Illustrations by Sam Thompson
Originated by Dot Gradations
Printed and bound in Hong Kong/China

05 04 03 02 01
10 9 8 7 6 5 4 3 2 1

ISBN 0 431 02317 4
This title is also available in a hardback library edition (ISBN 0 431 02310 7)

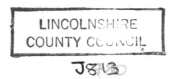

British Library Cataloguing in Publication Data

Lynch, Wendy
Dr. Seuss. – (Lives and Times)
1. Seuss, Dr. – Juvenile literature 2. Novelists, American – 20th century – Biography – Juvenile literature
I. Title
813.5'4
ISBN 0431023174

Acknowledgements

The Publishers would like to thank the following for permission to reproduce photographs: Corbis: pp22, 23; Chris Honeywell: pp12, 14; Mandeville Special Collections Library, University of California, San Diego: pp17, 21; Yiorgos Nikiteas: pp18, 19; San Diego Union Tribune: p16; The Times: p20.

Cover photograph reproduced with permission of San Diego Union Tribune.

Every effort has been made to contact copyright holders of any material reproduced in this book. Any omissions will be rectified in subsequent printings if notice is given to the Publisher.

For more information about Heinemann Library books, or to order, please phone ++44 (0)1865 888066, or send a fax to ++44 (0)1865 314091. You can visit our website at www.heinemann.co.uk.

Any words appearing in the text in bold, **like this**, are explained in the Glossary.

Contents

Early life

Theodor Seuss Geisel was born in Springfield, USA, on 2 March 1904. His parents called him Ted. His mother used to read stories and sing songs to Ted and his sister Marnie.

Ted's parents were German so Ted spoke both German and English at home. Ted's father used to take him to the park. In the park were **mazes** and a zoo.

Drawing

When he was five, Ted began to draw the animals in the zoo. He also began to read **comic strips** in the newspaper. His favourite was called Krazy Kat.

At school, Ted liked drawing **cartoons** and writing funny poems best. In 1921 he went to **college**. Ted drew lots of cartoons for the college **magazine**.

Marriage

In 1925, Ted went to Oxford **University** in England. Here he met an American student called Helen. Two years later they got married and moved to New York.

In New York, Ted began to work. He drew **cartoons** for **magazines** and for **advertisements**. Now he began to sign his name as Dr. Seuss.

The Tower

In 1937 Dr. Seuss wrote his first children's book. It was called *And to Think That I Saw It on Mulberry Street*. The book was **popular** because it had lots of pictures in it.

In 1949 Dr. Seuss and his wife moved to a house called The Tower, in San Diego, California. Dr. Seuss worked here in his **studio**: drawing, painting and writing books.

The Cat in the Hat

In 1957 Dr. Seuss wrote *The Cat in the Hat*. In the book, the Cat in the Hat made a lot of mess. Children loved it because it was funny and easy to read.

Dr. Seuss and his wife started a company to make books that were easy to read. In 1960 Dr. Seuss wrote *Green Eggs and Ham*. It became his most **popular** book.

Last days

Dr. Seuss wrote and drew pictures for 45 books during his life. People liked the way the words **rhymed** and were **repeated**, as well as the funny pictures.

Would you like them here or there?

15

Dr. Seuss was now rich and famous. In 1990 he wrote his last book, *Oh the Places You'll Go*. He died on 24 September 1991, aged 87.

Photographs and drawings

There are many ways in which we can find out about Dr. Seuss. People took a lot of photographs of him during his life.

Here are some **doodles** Dr. Seuss drew on his notes at **university**. He liked drawing better than studying.

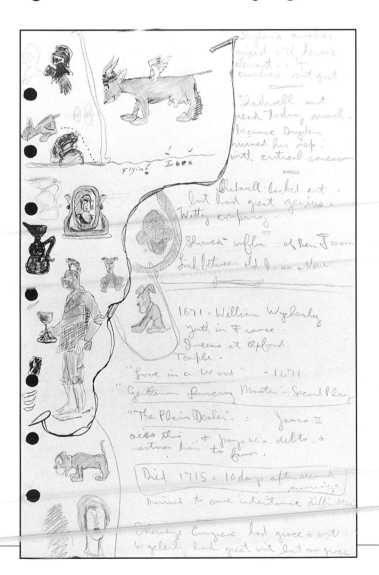

Books and CD-ROMs

You can read many books by Dr. Seuss. You can find them in bookshops or in a **library**. There may be some in your school library.

Books by Dr. Seuss can also be found on **CD-ROM**. It means that you can read his books or hear them read to you on a computer. This shows how popular his books are.

Newspapers and magazines

There were many stories about Dr Seuss in the newspapers. This story was written just after he died.

America mourns yooks, zooks and cats in hats

FROM MARTIN FLETCHER
IN WASHINGTON

AMERICA yesterday was mourning Theodor Seuss Geisel, alias Dr Seuss, the whimsical author and illustrator famous the world over for his cats in hats, fox in socks, scolding goldfish, yooks, zooks, grinches and nerds.

Mr Geisel died in his sleep at his California home on Tuesday night — a child of 87. The death last year of Jim Henson, creator of the Muppets, actually led the television news, but Mr Geisel's demise was considered almost as newsworthy in a nation so taken with fictional creations.

The passing of the man who invented green eggs and ham was prominently recorded on the front pages of almost every important newspaper. Experts in childrens' literature swiftly named him the Lewis Carroll of his generation. The newspaper *USA Today* even adapted his inimitable galloping rhythms to a versified editorial which began:

> *This is no time for fun,*
> *This is no time for play.*
> *Dr Seuss is no more,*
> *It's a sad, sad, sad day.*

Such was Mr Geisel's success and productivity that no two reports could quite agree on the bald statistics. Was it 48 books he wrote, or 49? Did they sell 100 million copies, or 200 million? Were they translated into 18, 19 or 20 languages? No matter. All agreed that the bow-tied Mr Geisel was the man who taught generations of children that reading could be fun.

He was born in Springfield, Massachusetts, in 1904 and had the run of the town zoo, his father being commissioner of parks. That evidently triggered his imagination, but it was not until 1936, after spells at Dartmouth College, Oxford University and as a commercial copywriter and illustrator, that he wrote his first book, *And to Think that I Saw it on Mulberry Street*, which was inspired by the rhythm of a liner's engines as he crossed the Atlantic.

Twenty publishers turned it down, but it became an instant best seller when it was finally printed.

He had no children, but two stepchildren by his second marriage, and told curious parents in typically self-deprecating style: "You make 'em. I amuse 'em." Mr Geisel's seemingly nonsensical books were fun, but often contained an underlying moral. The Lorax, one of his favourite creations, was an early environmentalist. *The Butter Battle Book* was a satire on the arms race.

Obituary, page 14

The Cat in The Hat, Dr Seuss's 1957 creation

Dr. Seuss drew many **cartoons** for the covers of **magazines**. You can still see these. Here is a cover he drew in 1932.

Remembering Dr. Seuss

This **library** is at the **University** of California. It has a room full of all sorts of things from Dr. Seuss's life.

The **characters** in Dr. Seuss's books are very **popular**. Here is a toy of the Cat in the Hat. Dr. Seuss will always be remembered.

Glossary

This glossary explains difficult words, and helps you to say words which may be hard to say.

advertisement picture or writing that tells people about a product. You say *ad-vert-iss-ment*.

cartoon funny drawing

CD-ROM shiny disc that can store words, pictures and music

character person or animal in a story. You say *ka-rak-ter*.

college place where people go to learn after leaving school

comic strip cartoon that is printed in a newspaper

doodle scribble

library place full of books. You can often borrow books from a library. You say *lie-bra-ree*.

magazine kind of newspaper that comes out every week or every month. You say *mag-a-zeen*.

maze lots of paths going all over the place where you may get lost

popular liked by many people

repeat when something is said or written over and over again. You say *ree-peet*.

rhyme when one word in one line of a poem or a song sounds like another word in another line. You say *rime*.

studio room to work in. You say *stew-dee-oh*.

university place where people go to learn after leaving school. You say *yoo-ni-vers-itee*.

Index